Sexu

The Inclusive Church Resource

DARTON·LONGMAN+TODD

First published in Great Britain in 2014 by
Darton, Longman and Todd Ltd
1 Spencer Court
140 – 142 Wandsworth High Street
London SW18 4JJ

ISBN 978-0-232-53067-4

A catalogue record for this book is available from the
British Library

Phototypeset by Judy Linard
Printed and bound in Great Britain by
Page Bros, Norwich, Norfolk

Contents

Acknowledgements

Inclusive Church is grateful to all who have made this book possible.

In particular we would like to acknowledge the enthusiasm and support for this book from David Moloney at Darton, Longman and Todd.

We are grateful to the Churches Equality Practitioner Group for ideas and suggestions for this book series.

We would especially like to thank those who have generously given of their time and contributed stories, reflections and resources for this book.

We are grateful to the Lesbian and Gay Christian Movement for their assistance with this book.

It is our hope that all that is shared here will encourage others to go further in the work of creating a more inclusive and welcoming church.

About Inclusive Church

Inclusive Church was formed in 2003. From the start, churches and individuals have signed up to the statement of belief as a way of indicating their desire to see a more accepting and open church.

The Inclusive Church
'Statement of Belief'

We believe in inclusive church – church which does not discriminate, on any level, on grounds of economic power, gender, mental health, physical ability, race or sexuality. We believe in church which welcomes and serves all people in the name of Jesus Christ; which is scripturally faithful; which seeks to proclaim the Gospel afresh for each generation; and which, in the power of the Holy Spirit, allows all people to grasp how wide and long and high and deep is the love of Jesus Christ.

www.inclusive-church.org

Introduction

*Simon Sarmiento has been writing about
the Church of England since 1998 and was
a founder of Thinking Anglicans in 2003. He
is a trustee of Inclusive Church and of the
Cutting Edge Consortium.*

For many people, Inclusive Church (IC) is
still associated primarily with the battle
against discrimination on the basis of sexual
orientation within the Church of England. This
is after all how the organisation began in 2003,
in reaction to the Archbishop of Canterbury's
withdrawal of the See of Reading from a gay
priest who was (and still is) partnered but
celibate, Dr Jeffrey John.

As the titles of the books in this Inclusive
Church Resources series show, IC has
widened its vision to address other forms of
discrimination in society and the church, but
on sexuality the Church of England and many
other churches have remained largely stuck in
the same place they were a decade ago. While
UK equality legislation has steadily extended

the protection offered to Lesbian, Gay, Bisexual, Trans and Intersex (LGBTI) people and other disadvantaged groups, church officials have consistently sought partial exemptions for religious organisations, in relation to sexuality, gender and marital status. These have been granted not only on grounds of doctrine but also on the grounds of 'avoiding conflict with the strongly held religious convictions of a significant number of the religion's followers'.

In recent months, after Parliament passed the Marriage (Same Sex Couples) Act 2013 despite strong church opposition, the Church of England's House of Bishops adopted, without any prior notice, a series of new policies that discriminate against all Church of England clergy, or prospective ordinands, who choose to exercise their legal right to marry someone of the same sex. This has conveniently exposed to public view the deep split of opinion that already existed on homosexuality, both within the Church of England and in the nation at large, which had widely welcomed this extension of equality.

Polling by YouGov in 2013 for the Westminster Faith Debates http://faithdebates.org.uk/research/) found that attitudes of Christians in England towards the family, sex and same-sex relationships have undergone a huge revolution within recent years. There is now widespread disagreement with official church teaching that sex should be confined to heterosexual marriage and that same-sex marriage should not be allowed. Each age cohort is less likely than the one before to agree with official teaching. Although same-sex marriage is still a step too far for many who otherwise count themselves as liberal on homosexuality, nevertheless 40 per cent of all active churchgoers and 44 per cent of all Anglicans are in favour of allowing it, and when analysed by age cohort, this rises to a clear majority among Anglicans aged 50–59. And in two years' time, these figures can only be expected to increase.

This book thus could not have come at a more timely moment, as churches discern the way ahead in terms of same-sex marriage in particular and sexuality in general. The Church of England has belatedly commenced a two-year programme of Shared Conversations on Sexuality, Scripture and Mission. As Steven Croft, the Bishop of Sheffield has written on behalf of the whole House of Bishops (GS Misc 1083, June 2014):

3. The proposal for conversations has two objectives, both with a focus on the

church's mission. One is to enable the Church of England to reflect, in the light of scripture, on the implications of the immense cultural change that has been taking place. It is common ground that social attitudes have changed extremely rapidly. Because of our calling to present the gospel afresh in every generation, a changing context always raises new questions about our missional stance toward culture. Clarifying how we can most effectively be a missionary church in a changing culture around sexuality is a key objective.

4. The other objective is to clarify the implications of what it means for the Church of England to live with what the Archbishop of Canterbury has called 'good disagreement' on these issues. There is no expectation of achieving any consensus – in either direction – in the foreseeable future. But there is a task to be done of encouraging those within the church who are at odds on this issue to express their concerns in a safe environment, listen carefully to those with whom they disagree profoundly, find something of Christ in each

other and consider together what the practical consequence of disagreement might be.

Susannah Cornwall's theological reflection titled 'Inclusive sexuality', which forms the main part of this book, provides an ideal resource, both for clergy and theologically aware laity, to engage in these conversations with confidence. Those in other churches, such as the Methodist Church of Great Britain, which are holding similar conversations, should find the material equally helpful.

Although some may find her approach intellectually challenging, 'Inclusive sexuality' is a refreshing change from the sadly repetitive series of official Church of England documents that have been published over the past twenty plus years, starting with Issues in Human Sexuality (1991), right up to the Pilling report (2013). She shows that a much more fruitful debate on human sexuality is not only possible but is already underway within academia. While still respecting the church's biblical and theological traditions, this work can be seen to be moving the discussion forward towards much more satisfactory outcomes, which also take full account of modern scientific knowledge.

Susannah also underlines the need for those engaged in such work to maintain dialogue with those Christians who reject the entire notion of inclusivity as a good. This is of course just what the House of Bishops means by 'good disagreement'.

PART 1
Experience

*Stories from lived experience are central
to this book. It would be easy to skip this
section and read the theological reflection
or look at the resources. The stories here
are real and speak of different people's
experience of issues related to sexuality.*

*We are grateful to these storytellers for
their honesty. Our theological reflection
and practical outworking should follow
from these accounts of lived experience,
so please take time to read these
stories carefully.*

Jo's story

Jo Ind is the author of Fat Is a Spiritual Issue *(Mowbray, 1993) and* Memories of Bliss *(SCM Press, 2003). She is currently writing a book on spirituality and midlife. She also specialises in designing content for digital media, having worked as a journalist for more than 20 years.*

If you can excuse me for using such an unfortunate term, there's something I'd like to get straight right from the start – I'm not excluded, or at least not in the way that some people are.

I'm married. My husband and I have a child together. We are a neat and tidy nuclear family, the kind that raises no questions and poses no dilemmas for bishops or employers or those who like to gossip in the school playground.

I don't suffer stigma. I don't live in fear. I don't have to endure people wondering how we do it. Were I to be called to ordination in the Church of England, I wouldn't have to suffer the indignity of being asked to be celibate.

What I have is privacy. I've got the ring

on my finger and the husband on my arm (or thereabouts). That means no one is making my most intimate yearnings their business.

But despite the fact that I am neither socially nor institutionally excluded, I feel diminished by much of what I hear on the subject of sexuality. The messages that we receive about sexuality from the world around – what's sexy, what isn't, who is, who isn't – leave me discomforted. The church doesn't help. In fact the church makes it worse. There's a dissonance between the story the church tells about sex and what my lived and breathed experience of it seems to be. And that matters because we need to know the truth of our sexualities in order to live them well.

Let me explain ...

One of the most all-pervasive notions about sexuality is that our sexual urges are all about the need to reproduce. In the 1970s, a way of conceptualising sexuality derived from sociobiology became very popular and is still very much around today. The sociobiologists claim that all behaviour has resulted from evolution. They argue that just as selection pressure led to animals evolving useful ways of interacting with the natural environment, so human behaviour is rooted in the need for the perpetuation of the species. We are attracted to people with whom we can breed and make good stock so that our genes will live on in the next generation. The attributes that makes us sexy are therefore those that show we can reproduce successfully. Big breasts are sexier than small ones because they indicate that a woman can feed her young. Well-toned biceps are sexier than skinny arms on a man because they show he can fend off predators. I've even heard it said by a sociobiologist that blonde hair is sexier than dark hair because it shows a woman is young and therefore more likely to be fertile.

The Roman Catholic Church says something similar but it expands upon it. Like the sociobiologists it claims that sexual urges are rooted in the need to reproduce. It says sex is not purely biological, but concerns the innermost being of the person. It says sexuality has a supernatural as well as a natural dimension. The Roman Catholic Catechism says, 'Sexuality is realised in a truly human way only it if is an integral part of the love by which man and woman commit themselves totally to one another until death.'

Other denominations draw upon the notion of gender complementarity in making sense of sexuality. The Methodist Church's report on *Marriage and the Family* (1992) says, 'It is man and woman together, as a single whole, who are

described as being "made in the image of God".'
Here the idea is that maleness and femaleness
complement each other and wholeness is found
in realising that. The Church of England
seems to agree. *Issues in Human Sexuality: A
statement by the House of Bishops* (1991) says
it's important that each person should come to
understand and to value this complementarity.
They too conclude that in scripture there is an
'evolving convergence on the ideal of lifelong,
monogamous, heterosexual union as the setting
intended by God for the proper development of
men and women as sexual beings'.

My problem with these ways of thinking
about sexuality is that they work with the
assumption that our sexuality is organised
around gender. The starting point of each of
them is that our sexual urges are rooted in
being one sex or the other. But what if our
sexual desires aren't related to gender? What
if there are dimensions of sexuality that aren't
to do with sex, as such?

I'm asking – I'm only asking – because
there have been times when I have been
aroused by things other than men or women,
times when the source of my arousal has been
prayer or ideas or architecture. It's important
to me to find a way of making sense of sexuality
that includes those experiences. If I can't – if

I ignore them or overlook them because they seem a bit odd – then I feel diminished and my sexuality feels like an alien rather than an integral part of me.

So what is my sexuality like?

At one level, that is quite difficult to say because it changes. I experience my sexuality as vast and rich and mysterious and multifaceted. It's such an amorphous 'thing' that it resists being tied down to one motif or two.

Sometimes, my sexuality seems to be right at the centre of my being. My libido seems to be an urge that's at the core of me, an overwhelming and overriding motivation and concern. At such times, I'm never far from feeling horny. The more boring the meeting or the sermon I'm attending to, the more turned on I am as my mind by default wanders into thinking about sex.

But at other times, my libido seems like a mere footnote in my story. There I am getting on with life, earning a living, loving my family and friends, gardening and singing and writing, and sexuality is just a little footnote. At such times my libido is either dormant or a little urge that adds a nice touch of spice and comfort every so often. That's all.

It's as though my sexuality expands and contracts and moves from the wings of my being to centre stage. All I can do is observe it, but I cannot control it. My sexuality is both predictable and unpredictable, rampant and dormant, mysterious and that same old thing that I've known since I first learnt to masturbate.

When I was in my early twenties, I experienced my sexuality in ways that were to me very surprising. I would be in a library working on an essay and I would get sexually excited. I would be in a church in a monastery, deeply involved in prayer, and I would become aroused – not because I was thinking about sex, but because I was meditating on God. At other times, I would be at a conference and get excited about ideas. There would be all sorts of different people from different perspectives talking about their research and, as I started to make connections in what they were saying and understand things in a new way, I would become animated and flushed – I would get turned on. Listening to music sometimes had this effect on me. So did making music. And while I'm quite prepared to accept I am unusual in this respect, I am certain I'm not unique. I know of a conductor who said of a piece of music, 'It goes straight to the crotch.' Naomi Wolf, in her book *Vagina*, has gathered stories of women who have been turned on by things other than sex. She talks about an actor who had an orgasm while she was onstage: 'Just from being in that heightened creative condition.' I have known women who have had orgasms while receiving communion or when glimpsing the castellated towers of an ancient church between two strata of mist on the Alpine border of France and Italy.

These experiences are not ones that I have every day, but they are sufficiently part of me and of my sexual experience to make me feel alienated by ideas about sexuality that are based on complementarity or attraction of opposites or forming partnership with people of one sex or the other. They have also been enough to make me find the Church of England liturgy around marriage very difficult.

In the Church of England wedding ceremony, the *Common Worship* Marriage Service Alternative Preface says: 'Our Lord Jesus Christ was himself a guest at a wedding in Cana of Galilee, and through his Spirit he is with us now.' I can see that this is meant to be a friendly way of welcoming the guests to the wedding, but it puts God in the wrong place, for me. It locates Jesus in a pew as an onlooker. He has the same status as the friends and family who are witnessing the vows that are being made.

The Preface goes on: 'The Bible teaches us that marriage is a gift of God in creation and a means of his grace, a holy mystery in which man and woman become one flesh. It is God's purpose that, as husband and wife give themselves to each other in love throughout their lives, they shall be united in that love as Christ is united with his Church. Again, in comparing the commitment that a man and a woman give to each other to the love of Christ with his church, it is placing God on the outside of what's happening. (Comparing the commitment of husband and wife to the love Christ has for his church has all sorts of other problems too, but they aren't so relevant here.) This doesn't work for me, because I see marriage as being first and foremost a commitment to God. It's a commitment to discovering the never-ending love of God through giving your life to a particular person. God is not on the outside looking on and blessing the marriage. God is at the centre, the being to whom the commitment is being made.

I think of marriage more like the way in which a monk dedicates himself to God through his commitment to a particular order. In the Benedictine Rite of Final Oblation, the monk is asked, 'Are you, therefore, resolved to dedicate yourselves to the service of God and humanity according to the Rule of St. Benedict?' So it is with marriage. I see my marriage as a dedication of myself to the service of God through the vows I make to my partner.

And I see sexuality as being fundamentally about my relationship with God too.

The Ancient Greeks gave us the concept of eros. *Eros* is the Greek word for love, from which our words erotic and erogenous are derived. It contains within in it notions of yearning and longing and holding all things together in unity. In the sixth century, the mystical theologian Pseudo-Dionysius, in *The Divine Names*, described eros as the divine longing:

> And we may be so bold as to claim ... that that Cause of all things loves all things in the superabundance of his goodness, that because of this goodness, he makes all things, brings all things to perfection, holds all things together, returns all things. The divine longing (eros) is God seeking good for the sake of Good.

This image of God is an echo of the depiction of Christ in Colossians:

> He is the image of the invisible God, the firstborn of all creation; for in him

all things in heaven and on earth were
created, things visible and invisible ...
– all things have been created through
him and for him. He himself is before
all things, and in him all things hold
together. (Colossians 1:15–17)

I see that energy – the source of all things that
holds all things together – as erotic energy. So
when we are turned on by a kiss, or a touch, or
the sight of a buttock or music or prayer or the
connections between things, we are taking part
in God's erotic work.

Put like this, there is no difference in
status between homosexual and heterosexual,
between the bums-n-tits-sexual or glimpse-of-
towers-through-the-mist-sexual. Put like this,
I feel my sexuality is integral. Put like this, we
are all partakers in the erotic work of God, being
drawn to the source of all things and through
him being held together.

Sarah's story
(not her real name)

Thoughts on being a bisexual in a Christian church or the ramblings of a Christian Grumpy Old Woman?

I hate labels and I hate generalisations. Gay, straight, bisexual, homosexual, transsexual, transgender: why do people want to put us into 'boxes'? They do it all our lives: boy, girl, child, teenager, adult, grown-up (don't know when that is supposed to happen: I am still waiting), parent, middle-aged, senior citizen, pensioner. I particularly hate the last one now that I am 64. People are living longer, more active lives now and I hate the way they lump us all together: 'pensioners', 'old people'; we span 60 to 100+, we have lives, dreams, aspirations. We are still the people we have always been, but once the grey hair starts to appear we seem to become socially invisible, unless they want to blame us for being a drain on the economy or try to take away our bus passes!

Wow! That was quite a rant to start off with! I feel better now. I am writing this because a very dear friend has decided to attach the 'bisexual' label to me. She is quite an expert in these things and has known me for many years, so, for the purposes of this piece, I will assume this mantle for now and write on.

A 'lesbian' friend once said to me, 'You can't trust bisexuals – no one is safe'! Well, since then she has been happily married – to a lovely man who has taken very good care of her. Labels – rubbish!

What qualifies me to be classed as a bisexual? I have been in relationships with men and in relationships with women. They have been a mixture of successes and failures: as I have now been single for over 12 years I wonder if I can claim any successes, but there have been successful bits in many of them. My marriage produced three wonderful children who have survived my haphazard methods of motherhood comparatively well and provided me with five lovely grandchildren: thank you, God! A later relationship with a man resulted in the birth of another wonderful child: thank you again, God! I have learned that the Lord can bring great blessings even from my disasters.

It was from 'discovering' that I was 'gay' that my marriage came to an end. I thought I had found the answer to all my troubles; the reason why I never felt that I belonged in the life that I had. Because of 'labels' I believed that I was, in fact, totally gay and always would be; I felt my husband would be happier when he found a truly straight woman. There was no one around to explain that being gay might just be another facet of my complex nature, and that there were other choices. My husband and I had no experience of this type of scenario, felt it was all 'black and white': 'you are now gay – move on'. It is so easy to be wise in hindsight. We were both so devastated by what was happening that we did not know to whom we could turn for help and advice; maybe there was help out there for us – who knows now?

Actually, there is a key in that last paragraph to the way my life has gone in general: 'I never felt that I belonged in the life that I had.' Hold that thought as I progress.

I was raised in a Catholic family. I had brothers and sisters and had a very happy childhood. It was only in my teens, when I faced choices about work or further education, that I realised boys and girls were not treated equally. It was considered by my mother that a university education was a waste of time for a girl; I would get married and have children and that would all be wasted. Women often stopped work when they got married, and if not then, certainly when they started a family:

that is the way it was – and the way my mother assumed it would always be. She didn't see the sexual revolution and the pill heading our way as I was growing up.

I followed the established path – job, marriage and motherhood, in that order as well. It was only when my third child was three years old that I first fell in love with a woman. I became a single mother; stage one in feeling an outsider in my church. No one was unkind, but I was in that 'everyone else has a successful marriage, perfect children' state of mind, so I isolated myself to an extent from other church members, although I did continue to attend Mass. What on earth would they think of me if they knew I was gay? Worse: what effect would it have on my children and their relationships?

When I later found myself attracted to a man again it was quite a shock: that resulted in a further pregnancy and the birth of my fourth child: now I was a divorced woman, single parent and with a child born out of wedlock! I remember attending Mass at times thinking, 'What would the Pope say? Would I be excommunicated if he found out?' Despite all the pitfalls and tribulations of life, my faith still meant a lot to me: I certainly wasn't a good Catholic but I was 'hanging on in there'. (I have since realised that it wasn't me 'hanging on in there' – it was God hanging on tight to me and refusing to let me go.)

I had now been 'straight', then 'gay', then 'straight' again: still unhappy and lurching from one disaster to the next. When my youngest child was about three or four years old I met the woman with whom I had the most 'successful' of my 'gay' relationships. We were together for about four or five years in total. Looking back I can see now why that one did not last either.

Back on my own again I finally went to talk frankly with my parish priest: he listened very patiently, showed none of the signs of shock or horror that I had expected. After asking a few questions, he said the following: 'You know that you are capable of having relationships with men or women. Unlike people who are either "straight" or "gay" you have a choice in which way you go from here.' I thought that over carefully, made a conscious decision to stick to men in the future, and went on to further disasters of the 'straight' kind.

In 2002 I made the decision to make the commitment to my Lord Jesus Christ and went forward for baptism. (By this point I had settled into a Baptist church.) As a mark of my commitment I ended the relationship I was in and moved forward in faith. From that point I have tried to keep Jesus in the centre of my life and make him my focus. Any relationship that might threaten that commitment is not going to get a look in. I tell friends that when God throws an amazing man at my feet, I see the hand of God pointing to him and hear a voice saying, 'This is the one I have chosen for you' – then will be the point at which I will consider a relationship and marriage again. I guess that means that I have made my choice at last.

So why am I writing this article at all? Basically because I have been asked to. What is my current situation in church? I consider myself to be firstly a Christian, currently a member of a Baptist church, but still with fond feelings for the Catholic Church, which I also attend occasionally for worship. Am I bisexual? Well, I could not offer any guarantee that I would not, at some point in the future, fall in love with a woman again, so maybe I am.

How does this affect my position in my current church? I think the biggest way is that I find it very hard to let anyone get to know me very well and this keeps me a bit on the outside; although I am a church member, take a turn at the tea and coffee rota etc. I have a few close friends who know about the paths I have trodden in the past; at least with them I can let down my guard and be completely honest.

I suppose this may all sound very cowardly to those who feel that we should be 'gay and proud'; maybe they are right. However, in my current church I do feel loved and accepted: I feel at home there in that fellowship. Being bisexual, or my gay history, still feels like a guilty secret: I don't want to rock the boat by speaking out about it. I also feel that it would place others in a position where they might feel uncomfortable, pushed into expressing a view or making a judgement about me – or about gay people in general. I know that there are some in my church who hold on to all the traditional views that come all the way from their Baptist childhoods. I will say, however, that I have been very encouraged by conversations that I have had about this with some very elderly members, so it is not directly related to age as one would expect.

I have invited gay friends to my church and they have been welcomed and treated with friendship, but they have been there as visitors. Those who know me know also that I am not in agreement with the church's current views on gay relationships and gay marriage, and that I wish we could be more welcoming to gay and lesbian Christians. I have not given up hope of helping my church to progress towards a greater welcoming of gay Christians in the near future, nor of exploring other Christian churches in my town who might be thinking the same way.

I have lived most of my life feeling like an outsider. This has been my situation since I was 11 years old and our parents uprooted us from the village that had been my home since birth. I attended a private convent grammar school on a scholarship; the other girls lived in big houses, went on holidays abroad, bought new wardrobes of clothes each season and threw the old ones away. That was so different from my home life that I just did not get drawn into conversation: my private life remained private.

I thought that marriage and motherhood would provide the 'happy ever after', and that I would be fulfilled and content. Being surrounded during the day by mothers whose only topics of conversation were children, husbands, what to have for dinner, etc., once again confirmed my outsider status. I was an alien!

Now I realise that we are all, in the end, outsiders in one way or another. This is probably why our instinct to 'belong', to join a group of people like ourselves, is so strong. Our need to be accepted leads us all into situations where to some extent we can lose our own identity, hide the real person God created us to be, in order to be loved and feel approval.

Whatever things are perceived as making us different from one another we are bound as Christians to love one another as we are. Whatever 'labels' we wear we all, and I do mean 'all', have things that make us different from those around us; each of us is unique and beautiful in the eyes of the wonderful God who created us.

Claire's story

In 1992 Claire took the significant decision to leave a successful career in teaching in order to change the direction of her life, which also included a change of gender and embodiment. This transition involved major medical, social and legal changes and led to the position where she is an active and respected member of her church and the multicultural community where she lives. She has just finished a PhD at Sheffield University where she researched transsexual transition and its effect upon familial intimates.

They say when you transition as transsexual it's as if you are reborn. I was born in 1949, so that makes me legally 64. But, socially and emotionally I feel like 14, the time since I metamorphosed into Claire. Everybody thinks that being transsexual is all about sex and the erotic; that's probably due to the fact that the sexual bit of the word itself is confusing. The muddle also arises because historically transsexuality and homosexuality were assumed to be the same and were often referred to as strange and queer. Sex is not my prime motivation because for me loving must be passionate, warm and a weaving of the mind, body and spirit.

What is remarkable is that I am still in love. Susan was my first teenage lover and Lisa my last.

Claire and Susan

My first memory of Susan was as a beautiful young girl with long blond hair, slim and very feminine. I had fancied her when I first saw her sitting at a bus stop as I passed by. We fell in love. I had a secret. I wanted to be beautiful like her and this was confusing. I was afraid to share this deep desire with her because if I did I was convinced that she would run away.

I remember Susan and me cuddling. I was able take her home after church youth club but I was not yet allowed in as her mother didn't yet know about us. We were young and in love and very close to each other, we stood that night looking up to the stars and shared our dreams for our future together and my calling by God.

I had learned from an early age that I was a boy and that it was absolutely forbidden for me to be a girl in love with a beautiful girl. I was a boy and must behave as a boy. There was another problem. I also had another girlfriend who was far away at college, and who was older than me. This was causing me great difficulty as I could not completely end it. We had been together for two years, from when I was 14 years old. I had learned since I was quite young I needed to have close female intimates.

Not long after Susan and I met we stole away to London for a weekend break. We felt so guilty and embarrassed that we booked separate bedrooms in the guest house near Paddington station. The reality of our shame was that we had to share a single bed in Susan's bedroom. That did not deter us when we consummated our love, a new experience for both of us. After two wonderful years of passionate love and intimacy our relationship ended. This was because I messed about trying to hang on to both Susan and my other girlfriend. It was hard to let go of either of them.

When I was little I lived with my parents in my grandmother's big house. I became a shuttlecock between my grandmother and my mother. I passed back and forth, bump, bump, bump on my bottom, between them desperately trying to please both. As a little child this was difficult for me to handle, trying to please my grandmother who lived upstairs and my mother who lived downstairs. When I got tired

I hid away in my little den under the stairs. Many years later, while in therapy, I realised that I had developed this pattern of needing two intimates at the same time, and this was why I had tried to hang on to both Susan and my girlfriend.

Susan was the first to get fed up with my arrangement and she started going out with an older boy who was far more mature than me. Susan's separation from me was finalised about six months later when it was announced that she was pregnant and was to get married.

Claire and Lisa

One early morning a few weeks ago Lisa and I lay entwined in bed listening to an online prayer resource. We engaged in a deeply religious and tender sharing of our forbidden love with the God of love and compassion. Lisa is a woman; I am a trans woman; I am 64, she is 40; I am liberal Catholic and she is Pentecostal; she is black and I am white. Her family would not approve of our love and intimacy. They see our liaison as one that will condemn us to hell and eternal damnation.

*

Lisa has gone and I am left alone. My heart has been ripped out and my compass, my soul, has been annihilated. The black water is threatening to engulf me as it slowly rises. What has happened to my life with her? Where are our dreams? Where have the laughing, the ecstasy and the passion gone? We used to pray to God entwined in our bed, but that's gone too. We travelled and danced to countries and knowledge afar, journeys rich with desire, fever, song and tenderness. The soul of two was nourished as one.

Grief is a funny thing you know, it's like riding on a whirling sycamore seed. Where is she? What is she doing? Why has she gone? What could I have done to keep her? Was I wrong or had I been too right? I am sad. I am lonely. I despair.

A couple of weeks ago I was given a black piece of cloth (a spectacles cleaner) by my creative-writing teacher. Black is the absence of colour, the absence of light. All has vanished, sucked into the black, black hole of the well, never to return. It is scary looking into a dark well. How deep is it? What's there? Is there a monster waiting to ambush your virgin body as it descends into the self? What will you find? Will it be worth it? My light has gone out and God has deserted me. Help, I need a light to show me the way, the path I am supposed to follow. No time, the descent has begun and the dark walls are flashing by as the fear accelerates towards the bottom; no brake can stop it now, too late, the dark is engulfing and suffocating the light of life. It is hell.

Yet up there in the distance there is a little round light, far off. How do I get there? Busy yourself and thrash about, that'll sort it. Join a singing group. Find more friends. Do some art. Sort out the Church of England and vanquish their homophobia. Psychotherapy and confession. Weed and prune my life or my garden. Give away my accumulations, that'll do it, it's certain to make me righteous. Fast for Lent and expose the atrocity of the need of food banks. Start a fee school and teach liberation theology. Just keep busy, use plenty of energy three times a day for the next four weeks. Come back if you need more. I know what I will do, I'll return to the cerebral and write academically again; that'll bring back the past eight years and distract my mind.

Of course I did not just end up at the bottom of the well, I was pushed or fell, not sure yet, but not for the want of trying to know why. I am struggling and gasping to keep afloat, to keep alive. Climb out, climb out, climb out and struggle up those slimy, wet, mossy, dark walls to a place of intimacy tenderness and warmth, a place beyond the present. It's not easy though because there is no route, no map if you're a transsexual woman seeking intimacy; the explorers who have gone and died before have not published maps of the route to love.

I have decided. I will trust God, the round intimate little light, remembering that we are always presented with choices in life. To stay at the bottom of the well is an act of grief and despair, a hiding from the painful truth of what has happened. I want to choose life and once more speak the truth to love, not an easy path to follow.

A few years ago a fellow explorer, a gay Jesuit brother, taught me the skills to make my own map of life's route. It is a simple technique drawn from antiquity, which is to review my life's past experiences and learn from them. So I set about dividing my life up into decades since birth to the present day. Then I simply recalled what had been life-giving and what has the potential to destroy life. In other words, what had opened my heart to God and made me radiant and open to all around or what had made me feel far from God, bitter and closed to other experiences.

So I revisited the results to assess my present situation. The following is what I discovered.

My earliest memory, at about three or four

years old, was of my widowed grandmother's lodger. Uncle Phil, who taught me to love growing plants. These were loving and positive times. The painful downside was that they had both died by the time I was 12 years old. The tears and anguish not expressed, as she lay in her coffin, remained for years.

> *Score: 2 to God*
> *1 to despairing estrangement.*

Janet and I really enjoyed passing secret, coded love letters under our desks in the first year at school. This was the time when I began to explore the love of the academic, the beginning of a lifelong journey of learning. The later reality of losing Susan and my other girlfriend (as I described earlier) occupied the rest of that decade, which contributed to the alcoholic disaster of university life.

> *Score: 3 to God*
> *3 to despairing estrangement.*

'I am pleased to offer you the job of second in the physics department at the Verdin Comprehensive School in Cheshire.' We left Wales for the first time and moved to England, that posh higher-class country over the border, the land of milk and honey. I entered a school and a teaching career I grew to love. I was married with two boys. I achieved distinctions in mathematics at the Open University and regularised my teaching career with a master's degree in education. The zenith of my teaching career occurred when I arrived at a brilliant comprehensive school in Nottinghamshire. I became the head of the science faculty of 17 staff at 28 years of age.

> *Score: 4 to God*
> *3 to despairing estrangement.*

By 1990 I was the deputy head of a comprehensive school with an exciting career, working alongside a far too purposeful Christian headteacher who was the same age as I was. Suddenly he died and I left teaching because I could no longer sustain my male life. Shortly afterwards in 1997 my Mam and Dad died having been in love all of their married life. After their death I began to assemble my new life as a woman, supported by a fascinating multi-faith rebirthing community in Sheffield. I lived embryonically nurtured in this group for nearly two years, to then metamorphose into a beautiful butterfly.

Score: 5 to God
5 to despairing estrangement.

The twenty-first century brought divorce and estrangement from my children and extended family. Retreats into the Jesuit community helped me to live on the edge while at sea in the storms. The wreck was rebuilt. The timbers were stout, eight years of love with Lisa and success in academia with an MA in identity and a PhD in understanding what had happened to my family.

Final score: 7 to God
6 to despairing estrangement.

So God wins, choose life and love again. I am still a 14-year-old teenager at heart and an inexperienced woman.

Martin's story

*Martin Hazell is a United Reformed Church
(URC) minister. Ordained in 1984, he has
served in Bexley, Islington, Haringey, and now
ministers in West Sussex. He was the URC's
AIDS Advisor from 1987 to 1992 and their
Director of Communications
from 2007 to 2013.*

Being gay has always been a part of who I
am; I have always known it. When I was 40,
my mother said she had recognised it in me
when I was two years old; and that was the
first time we had ever spoken about it. In my
first church, I imagined no one knew I was gay;
after all no one mentioned it to me directly.
But a lot of people assumed I was and spoke
among themselves. My moderator thought it
appropriate to inform my colleagues in other
denominations; he never spoke to me, nor did
he ask permission to tell other people. (This
led to some uncomfortable and embarrassing
conversations.) This inability to talk directly
and openly with me was very undermining.
Anyone growing up gay has at some stage

to confront their own feelings of shame and perhaps disgust. Silence makes this worse; discovering people have been speaking about you behind your back is doubly unsettling.

I know a number of gay clergy who marry someone from the opposite sex simply to counter not other people's disgust but their own. For most of my growing up I never tried to fight the fact but I longed to meet someone else who was gay and 'normal' and who wanted to build a relationship with me.

Arriving at a church with that sort of baggage is a vulnerable experience. I was ashamed and feared people's judgement and rejection of me. I chose to deny who I was; others act out with bad behaviour and some with anger. Those who knew and talked openly with me in my first church helped me to find some strength to face others. Through their love and care of me, I learnt to accept myself and become a better minister.

By the time I became National AIDS Advisor, it was much more widely known about me, and because I was responsible for education about HIV I felt it important to be as open as possible. Indeed, I often used it to prevent people, especially other clergy, from distancing themselves from 'these' people. But it did cause me a heap of problems – receiving hate mail and obscene phone calls from fellow Christians was in some ways the least of it; the URC made me ex-directory and my address was always given as Church House. After one difficult training day, a fellow minister said to his local colleagues, 'It's not personal, but I'd like to clean the floor with Martin's face.' That group put in a formal complaint and I was invited to justify my actions, of coming out to the group, to the then General Secretary.

Strangely, although it was a time when fear and hatred of gay men was common in society (the 1980s) and those of us who were gay found it a great struggle, it was also a time of deepening spirituality for me because I was having to address my sexuality – and for much of the time in public. I became thoroughly proud of being gay and determined to express it as a crucial part of my personality; and I wasn't going to let anyone persuade me otherwise or do anything to take away my pride in who I was.

My AIDS ministry shaped me as a human being and as a Christian, and accepting and being open about my sexuality played an important part in that development. How could it be otherwise: I was working among gay men who were facing certain death, sometimes in a matter of weeks following diagnosis. The fact I was open about being gay enabled me to get close to people in their fears and anguish. But being open within a personal situation of care and support is not the same as being open within a more public setting like the church.

Yet, it was that period of working with people with AIDS that forced me to bring my faith and my sexuality together; like so many gay clergy, I had kept who I was separate from my ministry. This became absolutely impossible while I was working so closely with men who were facing an early death from a debilitating disease. Stigma, open prejudice and fear were constant companions for many of those with HIV; how could I be worried because I was gay!

I remember, in 1993, I was asked to do a series of photographs reflecting my ministry with people with AIDS – it was an honour and the photos appeared in an exhibition of many other stories that toured various big cities around the world. To exploit the exhibition in London, it was opened to the media and the *Guardian* liked my story and interviewed me. The next day I was plastered over page five of the Guardian with a 'controversial' photo of me in dog collar kissing a very attractive young man. The article underneath talked about my AIDS ministry, coming out as a gay man and

the response of the church. I was honest and
open to the reporter and she did a good story.
Apparently the General Secretary of the United
Reformed Church on the day of publication
came into his office to find the newspaper laid
out on his desk open at the appropriate page
with a note suggesting that I be disciplined
or sacked for my behaviour. Fortunately, the
General Secretary thought it was the best bit
of media coverage the URC had had for years
and, no, he was not going to discipline me.

Early on in life, I found the road of faith as
a gay man a lonely and difficult path. My gay
friends couldn't see why I was still in such a
homophobic institution; my Christian friends
didn't want to talk to me about my sexuality,
well not often anyway. I have grown a pretty
thick skin, especially when, as has happened
in formal councils of the church, I have had to
sit through presentations where people have
said I was a danger to the church or someone
so disgusting that it sullied the church's good
name; and, believe me, some of the nicest
people can turn pretty nasty when discussing
sexuality in those settings. However, I have
not dwelt on these attacks as I don't think that
is very healthy for me. Instead I have brought
the question of sexuality into my faith. Not
because people have been particularly unkind

to me but because I have wanted to take my sexuality seriously and with integrity while also engaging seriously with the Bible and with theology. Today I am inspired by the many Christians who are gay, yet serve in ministry, in universities studying the Bible and theology and providing fascinating insights that have greatly enhanced my preaching.

I have been very fortunate that the local church, where I am known much more intimately, has been a good companion on my faith journey. It is always easy to be offended by other people's ignorance or stupidity but if you have a fairly healthy attitude to your identity then I have found, mostly, the local churches to be accepting and warm even when I have been bold enough to introduce them to new partners. I will leave to others whether I am any good at being a minister, but I think I bring sensitivity and an awareness of what it means to be an outsider to, what is, a very conservative institution. It is true that when I was called to my present pastorate some people left the church. It is hard to work out what they actually oppose in my ministry, but it has been more stressful for the congregation than for me. I think it's a pity that those who want to leave cannot find it in their hearts to at least get to know me; when people have stayed around and worked with me at their feelings about my sexuality they have accepted who I am, without necessarily wanting to approve of what they think I do, and great friendships have developed. I was very touched when an evangelical member of one of my churches stood up to someone who wanted them to support ridding the church of gay people.

My greatest challenge has been my time working in the URC's Church House. Based in London's Kings Cross, the 60 or so workers brush up against a multicultural and thriving Somali community around the building on a daily basis. It is not the sort of place where one might think people would have a problem with homophobia. I found it interesting that while I worked there I had more in common with black staff members, and many of the issues I found just under the surface were all too apparent to black people. There was a general unhealthy tone, but more disturbing was the unchallenged and open denigrating of particular staff members for who they were.

On one occasion I read in an email what one colleague had written about me; it was way down in an exchange of emails and I was obviously not meant to see it. Apparently my 'campness' had offended a whole group of people during an important meeting. I had let the side down and risked the project we were working on by being so 'gay'. Even so, this person, who was so angry with me, had travelled and worked with me for another week without mentioning it to me directly. And neither had anyone else mentioned it, despite the writer of the email assuring me 'everyone' was distressed by my behaviour. The message I took away from this exchange was: it was fine for me to be gay as long as I didn't act gay – don't be yourself, it seems to say. And isn't this what happens with some so-called welcoming churches – yes, you are welcome, but only if you behave like the rest of us.

As a final aside, around 1998, I applied for a job in Australia that I thought was made for me. The church advertised in the URC's *Reform* magazine for a minister to lead them in their ministry to the gay community in Sydney. I applied and was interviewed for the post twice, and then without feedback I was dropped and I never heard from the church again. Sometime later, in discussion with their General Secretary, I discovered I was not appointed because the church couldn't cope with me being gay – how they thought they could minister to the gay community when they couldn't even accept a gay minister made me wonder. I have learnt I prefer outright hostility to comments that are hidden behind friendship and/or a desire to be thought of as liberal; passive aggressive behaviour, which is common in church circles, is very disconcerting.

In general, over the whole of my ministry, I have been warmly welcomed wherever I have been. Most people have been interested and open with me and I feel at home in church and among Christians. Even among those who find me 'difficult', people are on the whole friendly and respectful. If people have been uncomfortable with me, it hasn't generally been in an offensive way. I think churches can be far healthier when they can be honest in their person-to-person relationships. I accepted a long time ago that not everyone will appreciate my sexuality for what it is: a part of me, but not the whole story.

PART 2

Theology

A Theology of Sexuality
SUSANNAH CORNWALL

Each book in this series contains a substantial theological reflection by an expert in the field. Here Susannah Cornwall encourages us to consider issues around sexuality, and what it might mean for Christians to be sexual beings.

'If we want things to stay as they are, things have to change,' wrote Lampedusa. Susannah Cornwall makes it clear why accepting same-sex marriage, so far from threatening the Christian doctrine of marriage, is necessary to defend and validate it in the present day. Being truly faithful to scripture and tradition means grasping that scripture and tradition themselves are the record of constant change, and so compel us continually to reassess and reapply their teaching in the light of new knowledge. Cornwall deals magisterially with conservative objections to same-sex marriage on the grounds of procreation and biology. She also insists that "good disagreement" in the church is impossible without honestly confronting the anti-LGBT hatred and violence which are endemic in so much of it. This is a perceptive and powerful commentary on a debate which should have been concluded years ago.

The Very Revd Jeffrey John,
Dean of St Alban's

SUSANNAH CORNWALL is Advanced Research Fellow in Theology and Religion at the University of Exeter, and Director of EXCEPT (Exeter Centre for Ethics and Practical Theology). Her books include *Sex and Uncertainty in the Body of Christ: Intersex conditions and Christian theology* (Equinox, 2010), *Controversies in Queer Theology (*SCM Press, 2011), and *Theology and Sexuality* (SCM Press, 2013).

Introduction

In 2013, Channel 4 (UK) broadcast a programme called *Sex Box* (Van Someren, 2013) designed, said the channel, to facilitate open and honest talk about sex. A range of couples – gay, straight, and of varying ages, abilities and ethnicities – took it in turns to enter a large opaque cube erected inside the TV studio. The cube was equipped with a double bed, washing facilities, tissues and condoms. Each couple was invited to go into the cube for 30 minutes, engage in whatever sexual activity they liked, and then come out into the studio to talk about their experiences with a panel of sex experts. By trying to 'capture' some of the essence of the exchange by virtue of proximity in time, the idea was that the partners would be more honest and candid about what they had experienced, in a heightened state of connection and openness.

But the most frequent commentary from viewers afterwards seemed to have been how non-revelatory the whole thing was. There was something about the dissection and attempt to pin down the specifics of what had taken place that failed to capture the emotional – and some would say spiritual – aspect of the exchange. Channel 4 may have succeeded in its mission to demonstrate that everyday 'real sex' was not particularly like the stylised, exaggerated pornographic version;[1] but what it did not communicate so effectively was such quotidian sex's deep meaning as affective glue in the lives of many couples.

Any given person's account of their own sexuality may be almost unrecognisable to someone else. As Jo Ind has noted, sex is spiritual and magnificent – some of the time. It can also be pedestrian and perfunctory; or dutiful and disappointing; or violent and coercive; or rendered irrelevant. Ind says:

> Sex is not like food, something we cannot survive without. It is more puckish, more mysterious, more will-o'-the-wisp than that ... Sometimes an orgasm is like scratching at an insect

[1] *Sex Box* was broadcast as part of Channel 4's Campaign for Real Sex season, a set of programmes that aimed to educate people on the nature of authentic and workaday sexual relationships in contrast with the version depicted in porn (http://www.channel4.com/programmes/sex-box).

bite. Other times it's like being rent
open and exploding through the cosmos.
(Ind, 2003, pp. 142–3)

Most currently or formerly sexually
active people will recognise the huge range of
intensity of physical and emotional sensation
that sexual encounter can provide, and the
pleasant, unspectacular ordinariness of much
of it.

Theologies of sexuality have often focused
on sexual ethics: questions of morality, of what
it is and is not licit or legitimate to do, and
with whom. We may indeed, and pertinently,
want to ask whether there are types or modes
of sexuality which tend to cut us off from divine
and human relationship: to be life-negating
rather than life-affirming, and creative of
exclusivity and division rather than welcome
and inclusion.[2] Less often, theological accounts
have focused on the cosmic significance of some
aspects of sexuality – in particular, marital
sex between spouses, and particularly the
kind of activity sometimes deemed 'real' or
'full' sex, namely, penetrative penile–vaginal

[2] Recent treatments have specifically begun to explore the
theologies of under-theologised modes of sexuality, including
sex work, pederasty (sex between older and younger partners), BDSM (bondage, domination, sadism and masochism)
and polyamory (see e.g. Jennings, 2013; Ipsen, 2009).

intercourse, the kind which may or may not result in conception. This, too, might continue to be an important aspect of the enquiry. But in reflecting theologically on sexuality and inclusivity, we may want to cast our net wider even than that. We may want to ask deeper questions not just about what kinds of sexual activity do and do not belong in the Christian community – and how some or all of our multitudinous sexual proclivities as a human race might or should be acknowledge or celebrated in our gatherings for work, life and worship – but also about what it means to be a sexual being in the first place, in relation to God and to one another.

CHAPTER 1

Sexuality and virtue

Communities of character

People of faith will want to continue to exercise moral judgements about types and modes of sexual expression, and may look to normative principles to determine whether or not particular behaviours are just, life-affirming, non-exploitative and respectful of the otherness of the other participant(s). One strategy is to weigh up every sexual expression against its likely outcomes. But an approach like this is unapologetically utilitarian, and may be insufficiently deontological (or duty-based) for Christians who believe that the Bible and the tradition have already spoken clearly and incontrovertibly about licit and illicit sexualities. The trouble is that each time and culture throws up new possibilities and new challenges – a set of new contexts in which the Christian path must be outworked. The Bible does not pronounce on the use of hook-up apps such as Tinder and Grindr, or the ethics of internet dating. It does not explicitly condemn paedophilia – indeed, we might be surprised if it did, given the prevalence of sexual relationships between men and boys in the Greco-Roman world. It is silent on sex toys and BDSM play, and muted at best on masturbation, oral and anal sex. And there are times at which the morality of the Christian tradition expressed in its past may be distasteful to present-day readers – as when Augustine holds that the continued existence of prostitutes is necessary in order that there be an outlet for the lusts which would otherwise unsettle society (*De Ordine* 2.4.12), or when Aquinas argues (on natural law grounds) that rape is morally less problematic than masturbation, since at least with rape there is still a possibility of the sexual act becoming 'completed' in conception and birth (*Summa Theologica* II.2, questions 153–4).

So we might more helpfully balance both the utilitarian approach ('What would be a desirable outcome, and what actions would and would not bring that about?') and the deontological approach ('What am I duty-bound to do and not do?') to sexuality with a broader, virtue-based account which focuses less on acts and more on communal goods. For virtue theologians such as Stanley

Hauerwas, the Christian community, like other groups formed around a shared identity in faith in practice, is figured as a 'community of character' (Hauerwas, 1981). The Christian life, such theologians suggest, is about the cultivation of virtuous character in oneself and others, and about building societies in which all may flourish and moral development may most fully take place. Virtuous sexuality (which sounds, on first hearing, po-faced rather than joyous, but perhaps that tells us more about the bad press that 'virtue' gets than about its potential) will therefore be sexuality which cultivates the formation of virtuous habits. And, we might add, virtue is about not just habits but also habitus: the values, practices and expectations we recognise as forming a good environment in which to be a flourishing human being – which, for many people, will mean an inclusive environment characterised by welcome and equality.

Sexuality, in fact, involves a range of interrelated aspects: personal identity; orientation to people of one or more genders or sexes; attraction to particular 'types'; arousal by particular activities, phenomena or situations; creativity, energy and interactivity with humans, other creatures, God and the physical world, which will be expressed genitally only sometimes if at all; and the kinds of people to whom we are drawn to build relationships of friendship and love (which are sometimes, but not always, also sexual). Sexual subjectivity does not seem to have been a constant across times or cultures; rather, it seems to have shifted and altered in response to social and cultural paradigms and modes of thought. Marriage has often not been motivated by romantic love or sexual attraction, but has frequently been a pragmatic matter based on economics, the construction of strong households, and the reinforcement of existing loyalties and associations. These have been particularly important in contexts where the population is at risk of eradication (which has also been an argument against same-sex relations: for the first-century Hellenistic Jewish philosopher Philo, men's sex with other men wastes semen, which ought to be being used to augment the population – Loader, 2013, p. 134).

Christian theologies of sexuality have, similarly, drawn on these various dimensions to greater and lesser extents. There has been relatively little theology surrounding 'types', fetishes and behaviours considered suspect, perhaps because of a strong emphasis on the links between sexuality and reproduction (with a concomitant sense that 'good' or legitimate activity is, largely, that which could lead to the conception of a child if contraception were not used; there is a small amount of reflection on non-procreative activity such as oral and anal sex within heterosexual marriage as part of a sexual relationship which will also include penetrative penile–vaginal sex, but this has tended to be limited mostly to Christian pastoral and marriage guidance literature – see references to examples in Burke, 2014). There has been a greater amount of theological reflection on sexual orientation, and a small but significant body of work on desire as broadly understood, and the place of sexuality and desire in the lives of people who are permanently or temporarily celibate and are therefore not genitally active with others (Gray, 1997; Williams, 2002; Rees, 2011). Being faithful to the Christian tradition means engaging with the breadth of this material; asking what inclusivity meant and how it was outworked at different times and places in Christian history; and asking whether there are some extant theologies of sexuality so exclusive and oppressive as to be reprehensible and simply inappropriate for today.

Being faithful

One of the most fully outworked accounts of sexuality from a virtue perspective is Margaret Farley's *Just Love* (2006), in which she argues that judgements about what constitutes good sexuality should be grounded in 'a framework that is ... justice in loving and in the actions which flow from that love' (Farley, 2006, p. 207). This takes place in the context of Farley's earlier work on the theology of commitment, and, indeed, she believes that commitments are acts of love, entered into freely, which come to exert a claim over those involved. Not every commitment should be considered healthy or unbreakable: fanatical and totalistic commitments may end in emotional damage and disappointment, and all commitments may need to be balanced against others on the understanding that one's balance of energy and ability to keep commitments may change. This should not inevitably be a cause for guilt (Farley, 2013, p. 2). After all, she suggests, 'what we call "commitments" seldom are, at least in our time, settled facts of our identities – not until they are lived to the end, or left behind for something better' (Farley, 2013, p. 14). Nonetheless, Farley notes, most human beings do still seem to be drawn to commitment to greater or lesser extents. Those who have already entered into commitments want to know how to keep them, protect them, make them more fruitful and life-enhancing, keep them alive (Farley, 2013, p. 8). The process of discerning when a commitment is no longer life-enhancing, and when, for example, it may be deemed no longer binding, is also a process of discerning 'the way in which grace works when it works in our lives of commitment' (Farley, 2013, p. 10).

Commitment in love is therefore also a significant part of what it means to love justly. Here I want to expand on Farley's position, and suggest that commitment in love, if it is to be inclusive, also means commitment to our theological forebears. But commitment to them does not mean never critiquing or resisting them: rather, it means engaging with them and the whole tradition seriously, considering it an object worthy of attention. This will mean neither dismissing the whole tradition as too outmoded and riddled with shortcomings to be perpetually useful for modern people, nor placing certain mores above contradiction and failing to interrogate their own genealogies and place within a broader religious, cultural and historical struggle. The 'argument from tradition' does not respect our forebears if it treats them as homogeneous or univocal; the 'argument from tradition' is disingenuous if it does not acknowledge the mixed and shifting nature of the positions theologically dominant at various times. Theological inclusivity means respecting persons, living and dead, by holding them accountable for their actions and inactions, examining the legacy of those actions and inactions, and asking what it now means to do justly. As Mark Jordan notes:

> Every new speech about Christian sexual ethics comes out of a library of older speeches. Before you speak Christian theology, you have already heard it. You have attended to the words of some scripture, of a local community, of authoritative individuals, of a denominational position or tradition. These words will repeat themselves in what you try to say ... Christian speeches about sex are full up with terms, images, arguments, and rules recorded from older speeches. These clips are remixed to produce new speech, which is sometimes music, sometimes cacophony. So speakers must be suspicious about how they are

repeating what they have heard.

(Jordan, 2002, pp. 1–2)

The capacity for change

Virtue ethics, and theologies informed by it, hold that social norms may be changed by, as well as themselves changing, those who live in their orbit. Too often, the church has promoted traditions surrounding marriage and sexuality as though these were (or should be) unchanging and existed as goods independently of the human beings in whose lives they were outworked. But this may fail to acknowledge how far the church itself has been influenced by, as well as influencing, prevailing moral norms in any given age. Individuals and institutions are often drawn to what seems ordered, settled, old, given or permanent. There have been huge, seismic shifts in western attitudes toward sex and sexuality over the last half-century; it is not surprising that the Christian church, a notoriously sluggish and unwieldy beast, has been slow to catch up. Francis Spufford comments:

My own church [the Church of England] contains actual homophobes here and there, of course, but it is dragging its feet primarily because it was so deeply acculturated to the world before the change. It had bound itself to the habits and outlook of that world, and those in the church who are the right age now remember the order of things in the 1950s as the old stuff, the sanctified stuff, the solid stuff, from which it is frightening and dangerous to move on. (Spufford, 2012, p. 195)

As Nigel Biggar holds in his critique of the Church of England document *Men and Women in Marriage* (Archbishops' Council, 2013), while there might in the past have been good reasons to oppose same-sex marriage, these same reasons do not necessarily hold water today:

In the past – both biblical and post-biblical – there were reasons: the fragility of human society in the face of natural disaster, disease and war; the consequent stringency of the social obligation to procreate; and the fear that the permission of homosexual relations would lead to widespread evasion of that obligation. Now, however, the future of society (in the West) is not (currently) so fragile … Divine commands and moral rules are not their own justification. Their only rationale is their service of the flourishing of creation, including that of human creatures. After all, the Sabbath was made for man, not man for the Sabbath.

(Biggar, 2014, p. 99)

So the argument that the church never has consecrated same-sex marriages before is not, in itself, even if it is historically accurate, a reason not to do so now. Biggar hints that continuity of tradition is important, but should not become a golden calf. It is just as possible to be idolatrous about good things as bad ones. If virtue means the cultivation of character, then character (both that of the church, and of those members who constitute and embody it) must be understood as cultivable: that is, both malleable and formable. There continues to be debate about to what extent sexual orientation is inborn and to what extent it is constructed by social circumstances, but regardless of the answer to that question, it is clear that social and cultural influences affect how sexualities are cultivated and endorsed. It may not be my choice to be attracted to men, but it is, to some extent, my choice how I react to the culture and circumstances in which my attraction to men is being formed and lived out, and the ethics I uphold in my relationships.

The church's relationship to the culture, on sexuality as on other matters, continues to be a tense and dialectical one. Spufford comments that this can be a positive thing, since the church can provide a check on uncurbed innovation-for-innovation's-sake and the damage it can cause. But the tension can also be deeply baffling and hurtful, as when it seems that the church is less morally evolved than the secular authorities. In 2014, same-sex marriage became legal in England and Wales. The House of Bishops of the Church of England issued pastoral advice to its clergy to the effect that no one who had entered into a same-sex marriage would be deemed suitable for ordination as deacon, priest or bishop, and no serving deacon, priest or bishop should enter into a same-sex marriage, 'given the need for clergy to model the Church's teaching in their lives' (House of Bishops, 2014). This caused much hurt and anger for many single and partnered, homosexual and heterosexual, clergy and lay people in the Church of England, some of whom felt that it was the final straw for their relationship with this institution. The first same-sex marriage of a serving Church of England cleric, Canon Jeremy Pemberton, took place in April 2014 (Davies, 2014), which led to his permission to officiate in the Diocese of Southwell and Nottingham being revoked (Brown, 2014).

For Spufford, the church's dialectical relationship with the culture does not excuse ethically reprehensible behaviour on the church's part; but nor, he suggests, is the church ever likely to 'arrive' at a comfortable relationship with the culture. He comments:

> There is no 'in the end' for human societies. So the implication is not that the church has to make its way through a finite menu of accommodations to social justice, after which it will have sorted itself out and become an institution in good order, which enlightened people can be glad to have around. There will always be more change needed.
>
> (Spufford, 2012, p. 196)

This capacity for change is vital, and is what individuals and institutions share in common, even if both often tend to the reactionary, the safe, the status quo. Indeed, we might add, the church's capacity to critique and stand over against social norms is part of what allows it, at its best, to resist hegemony and idolatry. However, the church also has a responsibility to acknowledge and repent of its own collusion with injustice.

CHAPTER 2

Sexuality and tradition

Dynamic tradition

Christianity's endorsement of embodiment and materiality has been continually present across the tradition, albeit not always expressed as unambivalently as it might have been. Opponents to developments such as the legalisation of same-sex marriage have sometimes claimed that these are ahistorical and do not do justice to the church's own traditions. But the Christian tradition is a dynamic one, in its accounts of sex and sexuality as elsewhere. As critics of appeals to so-called 'biblical marriage' have often stated, marriage in the Hebrew Bible is variously portrayed as polygamous (2 Samuel 5:13); contracted between blood relatives (Genesis 20:11–12); involving captive virgins who are the spoils of war (Judges 21:20–23); and a good outcome after a case of rape as long as the rapist pays for the woman before marrying her (Deuteronomy 22:28–29). Even in the last half-millennium of western Christianity, marriage has been variously figured as a sacrament; a social contract which is a pragmatic means to order society; a three-way covenant between God and the spouses; and a private matter concerning only the individuals. The consecration of same-sex marriages in some jurisdictions today is, almost everyone would agree, a change from what has taken place in the past:[3] the question is whether innovation always and necessarily means a break with or betrayal of tradition as broadly interpreted.

As Spufford holds, human beings often have short memories: it is comforting to suppose that things are done as they are done because that is the right way to do them, because the precedent speaks to more than just custom and taps into something ontological, unchanging and God-ordained. But the history of the church's

---

[3] In his book *Same-Sex Unions in Pre-Modern Europe* (1994), the historian and philologist John Boswell discusses liturgies dating from the eighth century onwards for *adelphopoieisis*, literally 'brother-making' ceremonies of union between two men. Boswell suggests that rather than signifying simple brotherhood or adoption, this kind of ceremony should be understood as a proto-marriage. Alan Bray's book *The Friend* (2003) examines rituals of pledged friendship between people of the same sex, and examples of extant tombs where such pledged friends are buried together. Most scholars have argued that it is anachronistic to consider such relationships closer to same-sex marriages than to covenants of non-sexual spiritual friendship.

teachings on and responses to questions of gender, sex and sexuality is more mixed and diverse than we may realise. Even in the course of the hundred years between 1857 and 1957, shows Timothy Willem Jones, the Church of England reversed its position on phenomena such as the legitimacy of contraceptive use by married couples and the acceptability of divorce and remarriage (including the marriage of a widower to his dead wife's sister). Surprisingly, perhaps, to many British Christians today, the Church of England was also vocal and influential in the campaign to decriminalise homosexual activity and understand lesbian and gay people sympathetically (Jones, 2013, pp. 162–82). Derrick Sherwin Bailey's *Theology* article 'The Problem of Sexual Inversion' (1952), a compassionate call for legal reform in order that homosexuality might be discussed openly and homosexuals helped appropriately,[4] led to the production of the

---

[4] Bailey still considered in 1952 that homosexual activity could not 'possess the significance that it has when it occurs between man and women" – which he ascribed in part to the non-possibility of procreation, and in part to the fact that it took place "outside the context of a common life of full personal commitment in marriage' (Bailey, 1952, p. 50). However, he was clear that not all homosexual activity should be understood as 'indecent' (he seems, obliquely, to want to say that although anal sex is indeed indecent, not all homosexual men – especially not those 'of character and principle' – engage in it) (Bailey, 1952,

Church of England Moral Welfare Council's *The Problem of Homosexuality: An interim report* (CEMWC, 1954). Despite its title, which sounds pathologising at worst and patronising at best to modern ears, Jones notes that it was a major forerunner of the Wolfenden Report and influenced the decriminalisation of homosexuality in Britain (Jones, 2013, p. 177). Jones shows persuasively that theological rationales for particular positions often seem to have appeared late on the scene, and are seldom unmuddied by less 'spiritual' motives (Jones, 2013, p. 118). On questions of sexuality, Christians often struggle to hold in tension what aspects of our beliefs are veritably

pp. 49–50). He concluded, 'We want the genuine homosexual to come out into the open, confident that he will receive sympathy and guidance from the Church, and a fair deal from the law of the land ... In a society no longer hostile or contemptuous he would find it easier to accept his condition and to make positive use of his gifts; he would be better disposed to benefit by psychiatric treatment, and his progress towards normality (if that were possible) would be facilitated' (Bailey, 1952, p. 52). Bailey's article was prompted by a letter to the editor in an earlier issue of Theology from a lay Christian, Graham Dowell, who had urged, 'The Christian conscience should distinguish between promiscuity and fidelity, between the balanced union and the vicious perversion – between, in fact, the invert and the pervert: it should then examine both the justice and the expediency of a penal code which, far from curing or deterring the homosexual, has so often led to crime (particularly in the form of blackmail), to bravado, or to the tragedy of wrecked lives' (Dowell, 1952, p. 29).

and characteristically Christian, and what aspects have other and more mixed origins. As theorists since the middle of the twentieth century in particular have stressed, it is not possible or realistic to suppose that we can get back to some pure or unsullied 'neutral' critical position unsullied by culture. Some Christians might wish that this were the case.

Doing justice to the tradition

The tradition, then, has not been static or unchanging. But the question for many Christians today is therefore what kinds of changes towards further inclusivity might be changes too far – and might betray the spirit of the tradition, or undermine some of the theological significance that phenomena such as marriage-as-we-know-it have been deemed to possess. In this context, faithfulness is important. When weighing up questions surrounding sexuality, faithfulness will mean both fidelity to those with whom we have sexual and romantic relationships and the others who are affected by them, and faithfulness to the (dynamic, shifting) tradition in whose way we journey. Christians' community of faith, after all, includes not just the other members of the Body of Christ currently living, but all those gone before us. They too are members of this (sometimes estranged and dysfunctional) family, and should continue to be conversation partners for us as we wrestle with how to be sexually faithful and faithfully sexual beings today. Inclusivity means engagement with the diversity and richness of the Christian tradition, past and present.

Being faithful to those who have gone before us does not, however, mean preserving a mythic prior version of the church by smothering it in dustsheets. Doing justice to our theological ancestors means continuing to take them seriously, and holding them accountable for how their positions have perpetuated injustice and exclusion (including sexism, objectification, gender violence, homophobia and exploitation) in the past, and may continue to do so today. Christians today will want to ask hard questions about whether the theological norms (which were also, in part, social, cultural and scientific norms) of our forebears in the faith reflect central and unchangeable truths, and to what extent they may be understood as patterns of belief and practice reflective of a different age and inappropriate in our own given the exclusion and oppression that they have sometimes perpetuated. How people read and interpret the Bible raises questions about their allegiances and traditions.

This dynamic account of tradition and our responsibility to it is also relevant when it comes to weighing up how the Bible may, could and should be used in discussions of sexuality. How do Christians live faithfully with their scriptural tradition, doing justice to the revelations found there, while also remaining inclusive of people whose sexual practices are apparently condemned there? And if scripture cannot be a sole benchmark for what constitutes licit, loving, legitimate sexual behaviour, how else may Christians gauge which sexual orientations and practices are or are not life-giving, just and worthy of celebration?

Some Christians wish to find in the Bible clear rules for sexual behaviour which may be applied in the contemporary situation; others have pursued broader biblical principles such as love and justice and have sought to work out how those should underlie Christian theological responses to particular issues (such as same-sex relationships, marriages between people of different races, slavery, warfare and more). Given issues of translation and chronological distance, it is often hard even to discern which biblical texts are talking about matters of sex. 'The pertinence of any particular passage to contemporary sexual ethics has to be established case by case, often at considerable length,' holds Jordan (2002, p. 23).

Ambivalent tradition

The trouble with transposing biblical rulings on sexuality too unproblematically into the contemporary situation is that, as Church of England bishops and priests discovered during the nineteenth and early twentieth centuries, the Bible itself was not always unambivalently 'on side'. European missionaries who sought to liberate indigenous peoples – particularly women – from what were sometimes figured as cruel or oppressive modes of sexual relationship could not always use the Bible as unequivocal warrant for their case. Indeed, John Colenso found in his interactions with new Christian converts in Africa that it was difficult to construct a univocal 'biblical' case against polygamy, since the Bible itself contained plenty of narratives concerning men who had multiple wives and concubines with apparent divine sanction. Colenso, a Cornish priest sent to be Bishop of Natal in South Africa in the mid-nineteenth century, believed that, rather than condemning the Zulu for cultural practices such as polygamy, these should be accepted for a time during the gradual process of their Christianisation. He pointed out that the Bible did not explicitly condemn polygamy, and felt that opposing it too aggressively would lead to the break-up of existing families, to the detriment of the women and children involved. Inclusion, for Colenso, meant the continued care of those who would be left vulnerable by a too-rigorous and hasty insistence on the ending of traditions of polygamy. As Jones notes, many European missionaries' opposition to polygamy was actually based in other norms, such as what would now be considered a problematic belief in the superiority of the white 'race' and of 'enlightened' and morally advanced European mores (Jones, 2013, p. 23). Sometimes this, too, was ostensibly grounded in the biblical tradition, such as the belief that the 'Curse of Ham' continued to rest on black people (see discussion in, e.g., Goldenberg, 2003).

Indeed, as the well-rehearsed example from slavery shows, many faithful Christians have held convictions which other faithful Christians find abhorrent, both camps finding warrant in the biblical texts. Christian abolitionists such as William Wilberforce and John Wesley held that the New Testament gave a clear picture of equality for all men (even if they could not yet quite extend this concept to women), and that there was no place for slave-owning in a body of Christ within which there was, per Galatians 3:28, no distinction between slaves and free persons. Other devout Christians, however, pointed to passages such as the story of Onesimus, who in the book of Philemon is sent back to his master with the message that he is to be welcomed and recognised as a fellow Christian – but with, at best, ambiguity about whether this should invalidate their concurrent and continuing master–slave relationship. Verses in 1 Corinthians, Ephesians and Titus urge slaves to obey their masters as part of their service to Christ. Furthermore, pro-slavery Christians pointed to various Hebrew Bible texts which exhorted humane treatment of slaves rather than condemning the practice of slavery.

Both pro- and anti-slavery Christians, then, sought and found support in the Bible. The Bible was therefore of ambivalent use in the quest to find clear and incontrovertible answers. Its interpretation now on contemporary questions of sexuality, as then on dilemmas of another kind, must take place alongside the witness of tradition, reason and experience. This is especially important given Jordan's claim that

Faithful readings of scripture treat the text as an occasion for divine instruction. The text becomes an instrument through which moral truths are discovered, constructed, and handed down. The text no longer contains moral teaching so much as it gives occasion for moral teaching. Different communities have received contrary moral teachings on the occasion of a single text, not least because they have expanded or supplemented the text according to contrary practices of interpretation. If the Christian Bible is and must be the foundation of Christian ethics, it is a foundation that invites believers to construct very different buildings.

(Jordan, 2002 pp. 44–5)

Interpretations and applications of texts on sexuality tell us as much about those who interpret and apply them as they do about the texts themselves and their authors' concerns.

Some biblical scholars suggest that, for people whose sexualities have been deemed illegitimate or even perverse on the basis of interpretations of the Bible, the healthiest response is not to seek to 'prove' that it actually means one thing rather than another (the kind of strategy sometimes employed by those who draw on social-scientific evidence to suggest that the New Testament texts may condemn specific types of same-sex relationship, such as those involving violence and coercion, rather than the kinds of egalitarian same-sex relationship possible in our own time), but to regard it circumspectly as something to be 'cruised' rather than considered a foremost source of authority. Timothy R. Koch uses this metaphor in his essay 'Cruising as Methodology' (Koch, 2001), in which he critiques three strategies often employed by (in particular) queer and LGBT people who reject the position that the Bible is condemnatory of loving same-sex relationships. These include re-examination of biblical terms which have been translated as 'homosexual' in modern editions in order to demonstrate that the Bible does not, after all, condemn all same-sex activity; disregarding specific texts in an appeal to Jesus whose love is enough to cover all and did not specifically comment on homosexuality according to the biblical texts we have received; and seeking queer 'ancestors' in the texts who might provide solidarity and hope to excluded people. Koch concludes that queer readers must weigh up the texts in light of their own inner self-knowledge, seeking to start from a position of certainty in their own legitimacy, and only then negotiate how, if at all, biblical texts may be useful. Queer interpreters must, for Koch, situate their authority outside the biblical texts and in themselves, rather than allowing the Bible to reign in judgement over them:

> Each of these three approaches still grants to the Bible the power to authenticate or authorize human beings, and, with that power, the power to direct my behavior and the behavior of others ... No, indeed. I name the locus of my authority as intrinsic, and do not look to these or any texts to be normative for my life or my ethics.
>
> (Koch, 2001, p. 174)

Many Christians will find a position as extreme as Koch's unsatisfactory, since it does not adequately seem to answer the question of why to use the Bible at all rather than throwing it out as something archaic and so morally reprehensible as to be useless, and because a position like Koch's does not carry a sense of scripture as particularly inspired, authoritative or revelatory. Koch's 'cruising' strategy – which finds among the biblical texts 'some friends, some enemies, a lot who don't care one way or the other (or else don't really "do" anything for us!) – and a few really hot numbers' (Koch, 2001, p. 175) – may, ironically, do too little to hold accountable those texts and those interpreters which have been life-negating and destructive to the community of faith, and perpetuated practices of exclusion. If texts are there to take or leave as we see fit, there is no particular reason to take any of them at all – or to seek on biblical grounds to question and query injustices and exclusions. Many theologians have sought to find a way for the Bible to be a gauge of accountability even as it itself is made accountable to the tradition, to the experience of historical and contemporary readers, and to the ongoing revelation of the Holy Spirit in the lives of the faithful. But always present in discussions about sexuality are the mores and agendas of the texts' writers, redactors, disseminators and interpreters, past and present. Certain texts have, suggests Jordan, become authoritative in Christian talk about sex not because of what they say, but because of what they allow particular communities of Christians to say (Jordan, 2002, p. 46).

Marriage, children and the open tradition

One important aspect of the Christian theological tradition's account of sexuality has been its frequent association between sexual activity and the birth of children. This has not been universal: most denominations now legitimise the use of contraceptives for family planning. Furthermore, procreation has not always been an expected or lionised aspect of marriage: at some points in its history, the church has privileged chaste, 'spiritual' or 'Josephite' marriages which do not produce children (Elliott, 1993), and from its earliest days Christianity has also held a high place for monastic communities and other types of community beyond the procreative. Nonetheless, many theologians, especially in the Roman Catholic tradition, have held that, to represent true and full self-giving sexual intercourse must be open to the creation of new life (which in this case means the potential new child of a heterosexual married couple having unprotected sex). This kind of theology underlies, for example, Pope Paul VI's 1968 papal encyclical *Humanae Vitae*: the deliberate suppression of conception means a selfish limit on self-giving. Even if sexual intercourse has other good aspects, such as its function of uniting the spouses and providing a healthy channel for their sexual desires, deliberately avoiding conception means deliberately depriving sex of its deepest and most profoundest meaning, that which is tied up with the actual biological destiny of reproductive human beings.

The Roman Catholic account is itself deeply rooted in the concept of inclusivity. Indeed, it widens the bounds of the community to be included beyond those who already exist, and stretches it to encompass, too, people who thus far exist only in potential. But the insistence that self-giving and openness to life always means openness to procreation is, ironically, a rather narrow account of generativity, fruitfulness and inclusion of others. Sex which is closed to life is selfish, runs the Roman Catholic argument; moreover, it is a disruption of the natural ends of the genitals and of sexual intercourse. However, one might counter, 'openness to life' need not always mean 'openness to the conception of a new human being'. Openness to life may mean openness to a broader community, which may or may not include the couple's own children (biological or adoptive).

Some theologians have countered that expanding the bounds of marriage to include same-sex relationships severs the link between marriage, sex and procreation. There is an expectation that the kind of sexual intercourse that takes place between a heterosexual married couple is the kind of sex that could lead to a child being conceived; it is for this reason, as John Milbank and others note, that in English law (the Matrimonial Causes Act 1973) a marriage is voidable if consummation (i.e. penetrative vaginal sex) has not taken place, and that adultery (defined as an act of penetrative vaginal sex with someone not one's spouse) is grounds for divorce. Where there is no expectation that sex can lead to procreation (as for same-sex couples), 'consummation' and 'adultery' cannot be defined in the same way. For Milbank, this is proof that same-sex relationships differ from heterosexual marriages. In the Westminster Faith Debates in 2013, he said:

> Immediately and quite properly we are recognising that there is a certain difference in gay relationships ... If we were indeed to abolish the difference then I think the consequences are very worrying indeed, because at that point one would have removed the link between sex and procreation. Sexual difference would have become completely irrelevant ... It's crucial that there is a natural link between the sexual act and the bringing to birth of children. This is what binds our

nature and culture together in the most fundamental way. If you sunder this link you reduce us to bare animality on the one hand, and to mere rational control which will be handed over to the state on the other hand.

(Milbank, 2013)

The Marriage (Same Sex Couples) Act 2013 does indeed set up a difference: a same-sex marriage cannot be annulled on the grounds of non-consummation (Schedule 4, Part 3). This represents a significant change in marriage law: same-sex spouses cannot be assumed to be sexually active, as heterosexual spouses have been legally assumed to be. But consummation itself is already an imperfect category when it comes to heterosexual marriage: the fact that the previous definition of consummation could not be easily expanded to same-sex couples is no great loss. Linking penetrative vaginal sex to consummation as the single moment at which marriage has, once and for all, been enacted, is deeply problematic, theologically and practically. It sets too much store by an action that can happen casually, abusively, coercively or violently. It denies the capacity of the marriage to grow, deepen and become enacted over time rather than happening all at one moment. It undermines the significance of a marriage ceremony's testifying to an existing relationship rather than being a moment after which it is legitimate for one to begin. Moreover, and not unimportantly, current legal and ecclesiastical definitions of consummation ignore the existence of people who, because their genital anatomies are unusual or atypical, cannot have sexual intercourse of the kind defined in law as effecting consummation – for example, some intersex people and some people with disabilities (Cornwall, 2010). Are the marriage relationships of people who cannot, because of their anatomy, have penetrative vaginal sex involving male ejaculation inside the vagina (which may include some intersex people, some people with disabilities, and some others) to be understood as inherently less veritable, less sacramental, less able to echo and communicate the cosmic relationship between Christ and the church than those of able, non-intersex people?

Milbank continues:

Allowing same-sex marriage is ... an undemocratic measure. No longer can people understand their biological identity as emerging from a human interpersonal identity, an act of sexual love, even if it's a one-night stand. You would also undermine the whole logic of Christian mysticism and Christian doctrine by getting rid of the idea that the sexual partnership mirrors the partnership between Christ the bridegroom and the Church as bride, and therefore you would undermine the logic of the understanding between God and creation where God has willed sexual difference. (Milbank, 2013)

But does sexuality expressed only in these particular ways, with their particular outcomes, really bind together human nature and human culture in the way that Milbank outlines? Does same-sex marriage undermine a shared human nature in the way he claims?

There are certain important chinks in his argument. The first is that it is already the case that not everyone is created via an 'act of sexual love'. Heterosexual couples who use technologies such as IVF (in vitro fertilisation) and ICSI (intra-cytoplasmic sperm injection) to help them conceive have already, it might be argued, interrupted the association between sex and procreation, even where the conception is still very much an expression of their love for each other and their putative child, and where, if anything, their pursuit of reproductive interventions demonstrates the depth of their commitment to opening their relationship to their children. The emotional, financial and logistical outlay that goes into commitment to conception via reproductive technologies might be understood as a practical demonstration of love for a person even before they have begun to exist. There is little romantic or spontaneous about this, yet it is undoubtedly an expression of love and commitment to a potential child to rearrange one's life for them before they have come into being. Furthermore, it is monstrous to think that violent rape could be considered in any sense an 'act of sexual love', yet plenty of children are conceived in just this way. Less extremely, where contraceptives are used, heterosexual married couples are acknowledging that their acts of sexual love signify more than procreatively. They point to their sexual relationship's capacity for bonding and unifying them, cementing a relationship which may provide an important rallying point of emotional security for others, whether or not they are the couple's own biological children. These kinds of cases demonstrate that same-sex marriage is not a sinister, shadowy entity coming to interrupt the pure and unsullied relationship between love, sex and procreation:

that relationship is already mixed and murky.

Finally, there is the important case of family formed via adoption. In the Islamic tradition, adoptive children are indeed never considered fully part of their adoptive families, since this would deny their birth family's claim to them: they do not have the same inheritance rights; they often keep their birth family's name; and women must veil in front of their adoptive brothers when they would not have to veil in front of their biological brothers. But there might be persuasive Christian arguments against distinguishing in this way between biological and adoptive families. Indeed, there might be good grounds for querying an over-solidified relationship between biology and family: the New Testament appeals repeatedly to adoption as a metaphor for reception into the family of God, with a strong sense that such grafting into the family tree is in no sense inferior or unreal. The thrust of Romans 8—9, for example, is about living not according to the norms of the flesh but the norms of the Spirit; Romans 8:14–17 states:

> All who are led by the Spirit of God are children of God. For you did not receive a spirit of slavery to fall back into fear, but you have received a spirit of

adoption. When we cry, 'Abba! Father!'
it is that very Spirit bearing witness
with our spirit that we are children of
God, and if children, then heirs, heirs of
God and joint heirs with Christ.

The biblical adoption metaphor is not a
perfect cipher for interpreting the present-
day phenomenon of adoption itself (not least
because it still ends up excluding some people
from the inheritance, and because in the Roman
Empire of the New Testament, adoption was
closer to the social promotion of young adult
men – often slaves – by elite households than
to the modern phenomenon), but it does at
least disrupt the idea that biological sonhood
or daughterhood inevitably and ontologically
'trumps' the adoptive relationship (or,
colloquially, that blood is thicker than water).
This is important, since, for Milbank, the
problem is not that same-sex couples could not
make perfectly adequate adoptive parents, but,
rather, that adoptive parenthood of any kind
lacks the biological family association which he
considers primary:

It's this natural act of sex that leads
naturally to children and therefore is
absolutely crucial in the continuation

of the human race, the link between
our animality and our sociality, the
setting up of kinship patterns that are
absolutely fundamental.

(Milbank, 2013)

But Christianity already testifies, through
its traditions of monastic communities,
sponsorship of orphanages, and frequent
facilitation of fostering and adoption, that care
and 'kinship' are about more than biological
relationship. The link between animality and
sociality is already a complex one – for we are
cultured animals too.

CHAPTER 3

Inclusive sexuality

Privacy and community

So how might inclusive theologies of sexuality be cultivated such that they are also virtuous and virtue-nurturing? If virtue is about the development of character in community – in dialogue with moral exemplars who pattern for us how healthy relationships and healthy sexualities should be, and with both our contemporaries and our 'ancestors' in the tradition – then it will be necessary to consider exactly who are the members of our sexual communities, and who has an interest in the way we conduct and order our sexual lives.

On one level, we might argue that sex is fundamentally a private matter, of concern only to those directly involved. The committee who produced the Wolfenden Report in 1957 said that homosexual activity 'between consenting adults in private' should be decriminalised, and that the function of the law was to 'provide sufficient safeguards against exploitation and corruption of others' (Departmental Committee on Homosexual Offences and Prostitution, 1957, p. 115), not to intervene in citizens' private lives or conduct. This indicated that even acts which might be deemed scandalous if performed publicly were acceptable provided that those who directly participated consented to them and that they took place as part of 'closed' private life. People deemed to be in positions of moral authority – including politicians, clergy, teachers and high-profile figures such as outspoken evangelists and missionaries – are often given a particularly hard time by the media if their sexual lifestyles are found to include infidelities, adultery, sexual relationships with those in their care, and sexual relationships which they publicly denounce as sinful. In general, however, modern western societies have tended to deem that what adults do sexually is their own concern providing it does not hurt or violate others or contravene the law. In such liberal democracies, pronouncements on licit and illicit sexual conduct from bodies such as the Roman Catholic magisterium have tended to look increasingly irrelevant. In contexts where the established churches still have more political and social sway, however, their pronouncements are not merely dismissed as curiosities, but may have continuing real impacts on, for example, individuals' ability to access contraception and safe abortion, or the safety of those who publicly identify as lesbian, gay, bisexual or transgender. There may be good reasons for holding that sexuality should indeed be a private matter, given the ways in which sexual minorities continue to experience explicit and implicit discrimination and abuse in churches and in wider society.

In common with several of the theologians I have already discussed here, however, I want to suggest that there is a way to figure sexuality as more than a private concern – while also taking a questioning, critical stance towards the pronouncements of church authorities who undermine personal responsibility and private choice. I am suggesting that this account of sexuality is, in fact, profoundly inclusive, since it means acknowledging a range of persons as 'stakeholders' even in private sexuality.

First, we might expand the bounds of the private community of sexual relationship to include God as well as the human individuals involved. For people of faith who understand sexuality as having a spiritual dimension as well as emotional and physical ones, reflection on the impact of one's sexuality and sexual relationships on one's spirituality will be significant. Where sexuality cannot be successfully integrated into one's psyche, this may lead to spiritual alienation and a sense that one is 'hiding' from oneself and from the divine. Inclusive sexuality therefore means not holding that one's sex life may be separated from one's spiritual and emotional life – and that dividing self from self generally does not have good psychological consequences.

Second, for many couples, their sexual community will include their broader community of families and friends. This does not usually mean that the broader community is directly involved in genital sexual acts with them, but, rather, that the significance of sexual and covenanted relationships reaches out beyond couples as isolated units. Many people will have had the sad experience of witnessing a messy divorce or other break-up of an established relationship, with its ripples felt far and wide. Where a relationship has represented stability and faithfulness, its gradual or sudden evaporation can be unnerving and disruptive for the families and friends of the partners, who may begin to question their own relational commitments. Such break-ups may leave friends and family feeling forced to take sides; in situations where the partners hold that the whole relationship was built on a lie, more people than just the partners may be forced to re-evaluate what they had thought were established certainties.

But the suggestion that one's sexual community includes one's kith and kin has positive implications as well as negative ones: it means that an individual's entire emotional and psychological well-being does not rest just with their partner, but has broader support and nourishment upon which to draw. It also means that there is a community of persons who are present to witness to the growing and changing relationship across its life. Such witness may involve a semi-formal promise (as in the Church of England marriage service where those present pledge to 'support and uphold the spouses now and in the years to come'). At a Quaker marriage ceremony, all present sign a large marriage certificate to testify that they were present to witness the declarations made. Even where there has been no formal public declaration of commitment, such as a wedding or civil partnership ceremony, each couple will have a circle in which they are recognised as forming a freely chosen relational unit, and in which their relationship is recognised as having significance for people other than themselves. If a couple has no relationships whatsoever beyond themselves, and no community in which they are recognised as a couple, the relationship is likely to be insular, and may not promote the broader flourishing of the participants, since there will be no accountability or gauge against which to measure whether the relationship tends to be free, life-living and supportive, or coercive, stultifying and co-dependent.

Third, inclusive sexuality acknowledges that sexually active couples are often at an age and time of life when they have caring responsibilities for younger people. These may be direct, indirect, economic, emotional, practical, permanent or temporary, and might include their own biological children and grandchildren; children they have adopted or fostered; nieces, nephews and other young relations; children of friends or members of church congregations or other groups; and other young 'mentees'. Established relationships may represent emotional, domestic and financial security to young people who cannot find these elsewhere; they may model caring, respectful, non-abusive and non-coercive relationships for children who have not experienced these in their own families or care settings; they may provide alternative safe adults to whom young people may appeal when their relationships are strained or untenable. Of course, not all sexual activity takes place in the context of an established relationship, and not every single sexually active person will have or want responsibility for younger people. Nonetheless, the Christian tradition has valued constancy and commitment as goods which provide stability for the whole community and not just for individuals or couples.

Inclusive sexuality will also take account of other invested communities, acknowledging that not even private sexual relationships take place in isolation from the ecological community, local and worldwide, or the global economy. Any individual couple's decisions about questions such as what (if any) contraceptive and safer-sex methods they should use, who (if anyone) should stay at home to care for children, who (if anyone) should change their surname upon marriage, and which sexual practices are and are not considered acceptable within their relationship are private, on the one hand, but always already political, social and economic at the same time. Inclusive sexuality also acknowledges that 'sex lives' are not easily separable from the rest of life, and that over-compartmentalisation may lead to an inability to integrate sexuality into one's broader energy and creativity.

Inclusive sexuality will also work hard to integrate a wide range of bodily experiences and sexual lives. This may mean an overt commitment to welcome and embrace a wide range of sexed and gendered body-stories (and a commitment to seeking out and developing generous theologies and ecclesiologies such that variant-sexed and variantly gendered people are not left feeling out in the cold, or either explicitly or implicitly told that their sex or gender falls short of a divine ideal). Inclusion may mean building in space for uncomfortable conversations, and acknowledging that not everyone's experience of sexuality is positive, but may include histories of violence, abuse or deep hurt. More trickily, inclusion will mean doing hard work and asking hard questions about what love and acceptance might look like when, for example, someone's sexuality is paedophilic. Inclusion does not mean inviting a known sex offender to become a children's club leader. Rather, it means ensuring that someone in this situation is enabled to find welcome and safety in the congregation in a way that does not compromise the welcome and safety of others. This may mean drawing up a contract which states that the sex offender may only attend specific services, or must attend with a chaperone, and must decline invitations to homes where there are children.

Inclusive sexuality?

Part of Inclusive Church's mission is to celebrate and maintain the traditional inclusivity and diversity of the Anglican Communion (http://inclusive-church.org.uk/about-inclusive-church). This means that its commitment to promoting inclusive sexuality faces another large challenge, namely, how to maintain relationship and dialogue with Christian groups which do not hold inclusivity as a good; which may, in fact, explicitly state that people whose sexuality is (for example) lesbian, bisexual or gay are disordered, and may preclude them from holding positions of office. Maintaining such relationships has something in common with continuing in conversation with our theological forebears: namely, holding them accountable.

Acknowledging a diversity of Christian convictions and acknowledging the imperfection and provisionality of all our understandings does not mean saying that all expressions are therefore equally legitimate, nor that every outworking of Christianity which seeks to situate itself in the Bible or in aspects of the Christian tradition is just. Being in communion cannot entail a failure to hold others accountable when their positions promote injustice and perpetuate exclusion, danger and even death. Western Christians have sometimes found it difficult to negotiate relationships with Christians elsewhere without repeating imperialist and colonial tropes. However, not holding others to account is not respectful or tolerant; rather, it is patronising. It paints them as people incapable of movement or change. It presents some cultures as static and stultified, in contrast with others which are uniquely dynamic and in process.

Imperial European Christian missions to countries beyond the West were, argues Lamin Sanneh, deeply liberating, giving those encountering the Bible for the first time 'the language of liberation and equality with which to oppose colonial repression' (Sanneh, 2001, p. vii). Once the Bible had been translated into vernacular languages, holds Sanneh, it became a means of political resistance. Sanneh wants to say that the Bible is not a univocal text belonging only to those in power. Sanneh's justification for Christian mission is that all cultures are shifting and in process. To paint receiving cultures solely 'as prelapsarian specimens of primordial purity and innocence which a herpetoid West proceeded to despoil with projects of exploitation, subterfuge and subjugation' (Sanneh, 1993, p. 232) is to infantilise them, to suggest that they are incapable of critique or informed judgement. The ongoing legacy of Victorian missionary teachings about sexuality can still be identified in, for example, the Anglican churches in Africa. But African Christians and others beyond the West also have responsibility, and have hard work to do given that Christian norms are often called upon in justification for the passage of legislation dangerous to the lives and safety of LGBT people – such as, notably, the Ugandan Anti-Homosexuality Act of February 2014. Acknowledging Christians beyond the West as equal partners in the worldwide church means asking how effectively churches everywhere are working to promote regard for human life and the equality of all people. Inclusivity may mean speaking with others with whom we disagree, but it also means respecting them enough to say, 'Injustice has no place here'.

Works cited

Archbishops' Council (2013), *Men and Women in Marriage: A document from the Faith and Order Commission published with the agreement of the House of Bishops of the Church of England and approved for study,* London: Church House Publishing.

Bailey, Derrick Sherwin (1952), 'The Problem of Sexual Inversion', *Theology* 55.380, pp. 47–52.

Biggar, Nigel (2014), '*Men and Women in Marriage*: Does it add up?', *Theology* 117.2, pp. 94–99.

Boswell, John (1994), *Same-Sex Unions in Pre-Modern Europe,* New York: Villard.

Bray, Alan (2003), *The Friend,* Chicago, IL: University of Chicago Press.

Brown, Jonathan (2014), 'Church of England Tells Same-Sex Married Clergyman Canon Jeremy Pemberton to Stop Leading Services', *The Independent,* 22 June 2014, http://www.independent.co.uk/news/uk/home-news/

church-of-england-tells-samesex-married-clergyman-canon-jeremy-pemberton-to-stop-leading-services-9555319.html.

Burke, Kelsy (2014), 'What Makes a Man: Gender and sexual boundaries on evangelical Christian sexuality websites', *Sexualities* 17.1–2, pp. 3–22.

Church of England Moral Welfare Council (1954), *The Problem of Homosexuality: An interim report by a group of Anglican clergy and doctors,* London: Church Information Board.

Cornwall, Susannah (2010), '*Ratum et Consummatum*: Refiguring non-penetrative sexual activity theologically in light of intersex conditions', *Theology and Sexuality* 16.1, pp. 77–93.

Davies, Madeleine (2014), 'Priest Marries Gay Partner', *Church Times*, 17 April 2014, http://www.churchtimes.co.uk/articles/2014/17-april/news/uk/priest-marries-gay-partner.

Departmental Committee on Homosexual Offences and Prostitution (1957), *Report of the Committee on Homosexual Offences and Prostitution,* London: Her Majesty's Stationery Office.

Dowell, Graham (1952), 'Letter to the Editor: The church and homosexuals', *Theology* 55.379, pp. 28–9.

Elliott, Dyan (1993), *Spiritual Marriage: Sexual Abstinence in Medieval Wedlock*, Princeton, NJ: Princeton University Press.

Farley, Margaret (2006), *Just Love: A framework for Christian sexual ethics*, London: A&C Black.

Farley, Margaret (2013), *Personal Commitments: Beginning, keeping, changing* (rev. edn), Maryknoll, NY: Orbis Books.

Goldenberg, David M. (2003), *The Curse of Ham: Race and slavery in early Judaism, Christianity, and Islam*, Princeton, NJ: Princeton University Press.

Gray, Janette (1997), 'Celibacy These Days', in Jon Davies and Gerard Loughlin (eds.), *Sex These Days: Essays on theology, sexuality, and society*, Sheffield: Sheffield Academic Press, pp. 141–59.

Hauerwas, Stanley (1981), *A Community of Character: Toward a constructive Christian social ethic*, Notre Dame, IN: University of Notre Dame Press.

Hensley, Christopher (2002), 'Introduction: Life and Sex in Prison', in Christopher Hensley (ed.), *Prison Sex: Practice and policy*, Boulder, CO: Lynne Rienner Publishers, pp. 1–12.

House of Bishops of the Church of England (2014), 'Pastoral Guidance on Same Sex

Marriage', 15 February 2014, online at http://www.churchofengland.org/media-centre/news/2014/02/house-of-bishops-pastoral-guidance-on-same-sex-marriage.aspx.

Ind, Jo (2003), *Memories of Bliss: God, sex, and us*, London: SCM Press.

Ipsen, Avaren (2009), *Sex Working and the Bible*, London: Equinox .

Jennings, Theodore W. (2013), *An Ethic of Queer Sex: Principles and improvisations*, Chicago, IL: Exploration Press of Chicago Theological Seminary.

Jones. Timothy Willem (2013), *Sexual Politics in the Church of England, 1857–1957,* Oxford: Oxford University Press.

Jordan, Mark D. (2002), *The Ethics of Sex*, Oxford: Blackwell.

Koch, Timothy R. (2001), 'Cruising as Methodology: Homoeroticism and the scriptures', in Ken Stone (ed.), *Queer Commentary and the Hebrew Bible*, Sheffield: Sheffield Academic Press, pp. 169–80.

Loader, William (2013), *Making Sense of Sex: Attitudes towards sexuality in early Jewish and Christian literature*, Grand Rapids, MI: Eerdmans.

Milbank, John (2013), 'Do Christians Really

Oppose Gay Marriage?', Westminster Faith Debates, Queen Elizabeth II Conference Centre, Westminster, UK, 18 April 2013. Extracts reproduced in Linda Woodhead (ed.) (2014), *Modern Believing* 55.1, special edition, 'What British People Really Believe'.

Paul VI, Pope (1968), *Humanae Vitae*, online at http://www.vatican.va/holy_father/paul_vi/encyclicals/documents/hf_p-vi_enc_25071968_humanae-vitae_en.html.

Rees, Geoffrey (2011), *The Romance of Innocent Sexuality*, Eugene, OR: Cascade Books.

Sanneh, Lamin (1993), *Encountering the West: Christianity and the global cultural process*, Maryknoll, NY: Orbis Books.

Sanneh, Lamin (2001), 'Foreword', in Vincent J. Donovan, *Christianity Rediscovered* (3rd edn), London: SCM Press, pp. vii–xvi.

Spufford, Francis (2012), *Unapologetic: Why, despite everything, Christianity can still make surprising emotional sense*, London: Faber and Faber.

Van Someren, Tim (Director), *Sex Box*, ClearStory Ltd., broadcast Channel 4 (UK), 7 October 2013.

Williams, Rowan (2002), 'The Body's Grace', in Eugene F. Rogers (ed.), *Theology and Sexuality: Classic and contemporary readings*, Oxford: Blackwell, pp. 309–21.

PART 3

Resources

SHARON FERGUSSON

*This resource section will help your
church consider how some of the issues
raised in the book can be taken further.
Here you find a glossary of terms,
resources and suggestions for establishing
good inclusive practice.*

*This section was drawn together by
the Revd Sharon Fergusson when she
was CEO of the Lesbian and Gay
Christian Movement (LGCM).*

Glossary

Asexual
A person who does not experience a primary erotic interest towards anyone.

Biphobia
A pervasive, irrational fear and dislike of bisexuals and/or bisexuality.

Bisexual
A person who acknowledges that it is possible for their primary erotic, psychological, emotional and social interest to be in either a male or female person, even though that interest may not be overtly expressed.

Cisgender and cissexual
This is often abbreviated to simply 'cis' and describes related types of gender identity where a person's experience of their own gender matches the sex they were assigned at birth.

Gay
(1) A generic term used to describe a person

whose primary erotic, psychological, emotional and social interest is towards a person of the same sex, even though that interest may not be overtly expressed. (Sometimes it will be used in conjunction with 'man' or 'woman' as in 'gay man'.)

(2) This word is more usually used to describe a man whose primary erotic, psychological, emotional and social interest is towards another man, even though that interest may not be overtly expressed.

(3) This word has recently become a derogatory term used to describe something that is deemed to be inferior, worthless, ineffectual etc.

Gender
The social division by which human beings are categorised as masculine, feminine and androgynous. It refers to those attributes which are culturally imposed and are learned through a complex and continuing process of socialisation. However, the terms gender and sex are often interchanged.

Gender identity
The way an individual understands their own gender which may or may not correspond to the gender or physical sex assigned at birth or by

societal norms. This may include identities such as trans, gender queer, gender variant, gender fluid, gender full, as well as male or female.

Heterosexism
The belief that male–female relationships are inherently superior, and that the only appropriate context for loving sexual expression is within a male–female relationship, the highest form of which is marriage.

Heterosexual
A person whose primary erotic, psychological, emotional and social interest is towards someone who is of a different sex, even though that interest may not be overtly expressed.

Homophobia
A pervasive, irrational fear and dislike of homosexuals and/or homosexuality.

Homosexual
A person whose primary erotic, psychological, emotional and social interest is towards someone who is of the same sex, even though that interest may not be overtly expressed.

Intersex
This is a general term used for a variety of conditions in which a person is born with a reproductive or sexual anatomy that doesn't seem to fit the typical definitions of female

or male. Intersex anatomy doesn't always show up at birth. In the past intersex people have been referred to as 'hermaphrodite'. The mythological term 'hermaphrodite' implies that a person is both fully male and fully female. This is a physiologic impossibility; however, some intersex people still use this term, but it is best generally avoided.

Lesbian

A woman whose primary erotic, psychological, emotional and social interest is towards another woman, even though that interest may not be overtly expressed.

Pansexual

A person whose primary erotic, psychological, emotional and social interest is towards any other person regardless of sex, even though that interest may not be overtly expressed.

Sex

The social division by which human beings are categorised as male and female. It refers to attributes and physical characteristics which are biologically related. This division is predominantly based on genitalia, however; even when physical attributes are not conclusive (see **intersex**) a person is still assigned as either male or female. The terms gender and sex are often interchanged.

Sexual orientation

A pattern of erotic, affectional or romantic attraction based on the gender of one's partners. This may be defined as heterosexual, homosexual, bisexual, pansexual or asexual.

Sexuality

Personal and interpersonal expression of qualities, desires, roles and identities having to do with sexual behaviour and activity.

Trans

This includes a variety of different terms such as transgender, transsexual, transvestite etc. It refers to anyone who transgresses the social division by which human beings are categorised as male and female. This may include hormonal and/or surgical intervention to change the appearance. Some trans people identify as the sex opposite to that assigned at birth, while others transcend the gender binary.

Resources

Since the middle of the 1970s numerous books and leaflets have been written on the subject of sexuality and Christianity. Some have taken a negative viewpoint, but many have offered a positive approach. They cover everything from theological exegesis to lived experience and now include workbooks for churches and faith groups to use to explore sexuality and how to become a more welcoming place for sexual diversity. It would be impossible to list everything that may be useful.

Consequently, here are a few more contemporary items that might be of interest and a list of websites where more resources and information can be found.

Books

Jim Cotter, *The service of my love*, Sheffield: Cairns Publications, 2009.

Rachel and Sarah Hagger-Holt, *Living It Out*, Norwich: Canterbury Press, 2009.

George Hopper, *Reluctant Journey*, published by the author and available from www.lgcm.org.uk , 1997.

Jeffrey John, *'Permanent, Faithful, Stable'*, London: Darton, Longman and Todd, 2012.

Bernard J. Lynch, *If It Wasn't Love*, Abingdon: Circle Books, 2012.

Alan McManus, *Only Say the Word*, Abingdon: Christian Alternative, 2013.

Oliver O'Donovan, *A Conversation Waiting to Begin*, London: SCM Press, 2009.

Keith Sharpe, *The Gay Gospels*, Abingdon: Circle Books, 2011.

Southwark Diocese Board for Social Responsibility, *Human Sexuality*, London: Southwark Diocese Board for Social Responsibility, 1995.

Unitarian Universalist Association, *The Welcoming Congregation Handbook*, Boston, MA: Unitarian Universalist Association, 1990.

United Church of Canada, *Together in Faith*, Toronto: United Church of Canada, 1995.

Websites

www.acceptingevangelicals.org
An open network of Evangelical Christians who believe the time has come to move towards the acceptance of faithful, loving same-sex partnerships at every level of church life, and the development of a positive Christian ethic for lesbian, gay, bisexual and transgender people.

www.changingattitude.org.uk
Working for the full inclusion of gay, lesbian, bisexual and transgender people in the life of the Anglican Communion.

www.eflgc.org.uk
The Evangelical Fellowship for Lesbian and Gay Christians. Welcoming people of all sexual orientations and any gender identity.

www.gaychristian.net
A Christian ministry dedicated to building bridges and offering support. Helps create safe spaces both online and offline for Christians of all sorts to make friends, ask questions, get support and offer support to others.

www.gaychristian101.com
A website giving voice to Bible-believing conservative gay evangelicals.

www.gaychurch.org
Ministering to the LGBT Christian community, this website features the largest welcoming and Affirming Church Directory in the world.

www.lesbepure.com
Online resources for the LGBT community, with a focus on lesbian issues.

www.left101.weebly.com
For lesbian and bisexual women exploring faith.

www.lgcm.org.uk
UK-based international charity which challenges homophobia and transphobia, especially within

the church and faith-based organisations, as well as working to create and praying for an inclusive church.

www.mcchurch.org
Metropolitan Community Church is a global church with a specific and intentional outreach to/with homosexual, bisexual and transgender people. MCC churches actively minister in their communities to and with LGBT (lesbian, gay, bisexual, transgender) people.

www.sibyls.co.uk
A UK-based confidential Christian spirituality group for transgender people and their supporters, offering companionship along the journey, and information/advocacy to churches.

www.welcomingresources.org
The Institute for Welcoming Resources providing resources, conferences and training for churches seeking to be welcoming and inclusive of LGBT people.

Inclusive practice

All congregations are made up of a diverse group of people: some differences are obvious, some differences challenge us, some differences require us to take action, and some differences we choose to ignore.

For all of us to feel welcomed and included in a group of people we need to feel we are 'seen', understood and accepted for who we are. If you identify with a minority group it can often feel that asking for what others take for granted is an imposition and a burden, and so we remain silent. The downside of this is that those from the majority group can remain completely unaware of the need for change or the effect their current behaviour has on a person. Open, honest dialogue is always the only way forward.

Your congregation may have already signed up to inclusive practices or already held some conversations around being more welcoming to minority groups. Alternatively, your congregation may feel there is no need for any of this; they don't have people like that in their church so it's not necessary.

The reality is that just as not all disabilities are immediately apparent neither are all lesbian, gay, bisexual or trans people.

Jesus made it abundantly clear that *all* are welcome. Our churches should reflect this. If you really don't have any LGBT people attending your church perhaps you should start with exploring why this might be. Does your website reflect that LGBT people would be welcome? Do you have any positive literature available to take away in your church? What do you say in your liturgy?

There are a number of resources available that offer workshop guidelines to explore issues of human sexuality, with suggestions for actions you can take to make your church more welcoming. These vary in length, duration and cost.

If finance is an issue for your church there are still many things that you can do.

- Invite LGBT Christians to share their faith story either in church or at a midweek group.
- Invite the parent(s) of an LGBT child to share their journey of acceptance.
- Ask LGBT faith organisations to send you some leaflets, membership forms, posters etc.

All these things will help to generate conversation.

With a few resources from some of the organisations listed above you can also design your own workshops. The main topics you will want to cover are:

- Sexuality and gender diversity – theology, biology, psychology and society.

- Justice issues – persecution, discrimination, mixed messages.
- The costs of heterosexism and homophobia, biphobia and transphobia – how are you falling short of Christ's command to love your neighbour as yourself?
- Strategy for inclusion, including the use of language – what assumptions do you make? What needs to change?

Being inclusive is not a one-off achievement, it is a journey which needs constant review. Our congregations are also not static and therefore conversations need to be repeated regularly to allow everyone the opportunity to participate.

Index